COMING TO AMERICA

A Stage 3
Newbury House Reader

COMING TO AMERICA

Adapted by
Bruce Coleman
and
Josephine Hileman

NEWBURY HOUSE PUBLISHERS, Cambridge
A division of Harper & Row, Publishers, Inc.
New York, Philadelphia, San Francisco, Washington
London, Mexico City, São Paulo, Singapore, Sydney

Library of Congress Cataloging in Publication Data

Main entry under title:

Coming to America.

   (Newbury House readers series: Stage 3)
    1. English language--Text-books for foreigners.
2. Readers--1950-   . 3. San Francisco--Foreign
population. I. Coleman, Bruce. II. Hileman,
Josephine.
PE1128.C693   428.6'4   80-28170
ISBN 0-88377-196-9

Photos by James De Noon

Original drawings by Margaret Leach, Peter A. Linenthal, and Youngmi Choi

NEWBURY HOUSE PUBLISHERS
A division of Harper & Row, Publishers, Inc.

 Language Science
Language Teaching
Language Learning

CAMBRIDGE, MASSACHUSETTS

Printed in the U.S.A.

                    First printing: February 1981

To
the Coleman and Lewis clans

Contents

Introduction

The stories in *Coming to America* are by students of Alemany Community College Center of the San Francisco Community College District, San Francisco.

The names of the students are fictitious. However, the true name of the student's country has been used to identify his or her ethnic background.

Many of these stories originally appeared in the student newspaper, *The Alemany Gazette.*

1.
A Bad Day

I can remember March 8, 1964, in Beijing, China. It was dark and moonless in the middle of the night. When all the people were asleep, the earthquake came. All the people got excited.

My two friends, Mr. Lee who was tall, and Mr. Long who was short, were sleeping in one bed together. The television told all the people to be careful to prevent injuries in the earthquake. So they slept with their coats and pants under their pillows.

When the earthquake started, Mr. Long was so afraid that he hid under the table. But then he put on the wrong pants — Mr. Lee's. Mr. Lee tried to wear Mr. Long's pants, but he couldn't get them on, and the weather was very cold.

This was a bad day in Beijing, China.

— Ming (China)

3

2.
A Good Day

Last year I was in Korea. The girl I will marry was there, too. We had a very happy day. We went to the beach and the mountains. She cooked and I sang. Nobody saw us if we kissed. We were very happy. She said, "You are my world."

I said, "I am a very lucky man." So I sang all the time. After that we kissed for a very long time.

She was a lucky girl because she caught me.

— Kim (Korea)

3.
A Bad Night

Tomorrow night will be a bad night for me. I say this for two reasons. The first one is because tomorrow will be my birthday and I feel old. I want to do everything fast before time catches up with me.

The second reason is because tomorrow night I have to work with my partners and we have to serve almost 1,000 dishes. I'll work very hard.

Some people who are in Peru think that tomorrow night I'll be enjoying music at a party. Some people believe that people who come to the USA have it very easy. They think that money comes from the sky. I say that some people don't know what our real problems in life are.

— Roberto (Peru)

4.
A Good
and Bad Day

I left my country last July 25. It was a bad day because my boat broke down on the ocean. We were very worried. We didn't have any water on the boat so we were very thirsty and hungry. I was very sad. I thought maybe I would die later.

After 10 days on the ocean, one day we saw a ship in front of us but very far away from ours. This ship slowly came near my boat. Then the people on the ship helped us.

We survived after a very long, terrible day. So, in the end, it was a good day.

— Thieu (Viet Nam)

EXERCISE 1

Choose the correct answer: (a), (b), or (c).

1. In story number 1, people got excited because (a) there was a storm, (b) there was a flood, (c) there was a movement of the earth.
2. In story 1, the men (a) slept in the same bed, (b) slept in separate beds, (c) slept on pillows on the floor.
3. In story 1, the two men went to bed (a) in their pajamas, (b) wearing their pants, (c) with their pants under their pillows.
4. In story 1, the earthquake came (a) at about midnight, (b) at sunrise, (c) in the middle of the day.
5. In story 2, the young man and the young woman were in (a) Hong Kong, (b) San Francisco, (c) Korea.
6. In story 2, the young man (a) liked to sing, (b) liked to play the guitar, (c) liked to cook.
7. In story 3, Roberto was (a) going to a birthday party, (b) going to work, (c) going to his friend's house.
8. In story 3, Roberto said that he felt (a) old, (b) very happy because his birthday was tomorrow, (c) very tired.
9. In story number 4, Thieu saw a ship (a) on the same day, (b) after 10 days, (c) on July 25.
10. In story 4, Thieu was very thirsty. She couldn't drink water because (a) the water was bad, (b) the water was too old, (c) there was no water to drink.

EXERCISE 2 (Writing)

Think about a good day or a bad day in your life. For example, think about last weekend. Why was Saturday or Sunday good? Why was one day bad? Now write three or four sentences telling your classmates and teacher about that day.

Coming to America

There were many families waiting for the important answer. They were waiting to find out if they had the O.K. to go to the U.S.

Everybody at the U.S. Office in Bogota, Colombia, had put on their best clothes. And quite a few ladies had been in the beauty shop all morning.

Finally at 10 p.m., when everybody was sleeping, the American Consul telephoned my mother, my sister, and me. We were so nervous. At the same time, we were so calm because we knew we had done everything perfectly.

We went to the Consul's office. The Consul asked us why we wanted to go to the United States. He asked us if we were going to work. He asked us if we had relatives who would be waiting for us at the airport in the United States. And he asked other questions that I don't remember right now. After 30 minutes, he said, "Yes, you can go to the United States!!"

Oh, God, it was a happy night! When we left the office everybody was very quiet. When we got home our friends and relatives were waiting for our answer. But we didn't have to say anything because the answer was on our faces.

And here I am.

— Ana (Colombia)

Arriving in America

After sitting in the airplane for about fourteen hours, I got to San Francisco International Airport at 8:30 a.m., September 29. Right away, I put my tired body in my brother-in-law's car to drive to his home. On the way, I saw highways like I'd never seen before. The traffic was moving slowly, and it took about forty-five minutes to get to his home.

Then we went to a Chinese tea house. After eating something, I felt the taste was not as good as Hong Kong's food.

Later we went to Chinatown. When we arrived, I saw the houses are very old and dirty. That made me feel I had come to China, not the United States.

I found out that I couldn't buy many kinds of things that I was used to. Either they were not on sale in the United States or they were too expensive. But I did buy many cheap and delicious fruits here. I was thankful for that because I like fruit.

I had thought that after I visited all the interesting things in San Francisco, I would find a good job. But I found out that I was wrong. Except for working in Chinese restaurants, finding a job isn't easy. I was disappointed.

Also, I wasn't used to the cold weather, and I wasn't used to speaking English outside. I wanted to go back to Hong Kong. But I have a chance to improve my English. I hope my English gets better. I hope time will change my mind about staying in the United States.

— Kwok (Hong Kong)

EXERCISE 1

Use the word THE where necessary.

Ana, her mother, and Ana's sister wanted to go to (1) _____ United States. They were living in (2) _____ Colombia. There were many other (3) _____ people who wanted to go, too.

(4) _____ interviews were made with (5) _____ U.S. Consul's office. (6) _____ applications were filled out. Ana and her family applied for (7) _____ passports. Before going to the Consul's office, some women went to (8) _____ beauty shop to get their hair fixed. They were there in (9) _____ morning. (10) _____ women thought it would be helpful if they looked pretty.

EXERCISE 2 (Writing)

Write two or three sentences about what you did to get ready to come to the United States. What did you have to do? Did you have to pack your things in suitcases? Who came with you?

EXERCISE 3

Answer the questions in complete sentences.

1. How did Kwok feel when he got into his brother-in-law's car?
2. What did Kwok think about the food at the Chinese tea house?
3. How did Kwok feel about Chinatown?
4. Why couldn't Kwok buy everything he wanted?
5. Where could Kwok get a job? Did he want that job?
6. What are two other things Kwok wasn't used to?
7. How does Kwok feel about the United States?
8. What does he hope will make him want to stay in the United States?
9. What was the only thing Kwok liked doing in the United States?

How did you feel?

Tell your classmates the answers to these questions.

1. How did you feel when you first came to the United States?
2. How did your feelings change?
3. What helped you feel good?
4. If you could talk to Kwok, what would you tell him?

12

Welcome

My sister-in-law, Sarah, is an American from Boston. I thought I knew American people a little. I thought there were not many differences. So I didn't worry about that.

I went to my landlord's house in San Francisco the day after I arrived in the USA. They said, "How do you do, Kimiko." Then they squeezed me and kissed me. I was very surprised and felt no good. Sarah never did that and neither did Sarah's mother. I can understand now they showed me "welcome" and there is a difference between Boston and San Francisco.

— Kimiko (Japan)

Living in America

All people who live in a new country must adjust to a new culture. I have lived in the USA nearly five months. Here are some things that I have learned about American ways.

Americans always smile modestly and say, "thank you," when you say that you enjoyed their food. On the other hand, you can't be modest about your abilities. Then the American employers think you are not good at what you do.

When friends "eat out" together, each person orders whatever he wants to eat. Then each person pays for his own food. This is known as "Dutch treat." This custom helps someone who can't spend too much money when he eats in a restaurant with his friends.

Don't be surprised that the Americans prefer not to live with their children when they are in old age. That is because Americans want personal independence. That doesn't mean that their children don't love them.

Don't ask Americans, "How old are you?" They will not want to answer this question, especially women. They will not want to tell their ages.

Don't be surprised to see American husbands take care of the baby or cook in the kitchen, and American wives do "men's work." For example, a woman drives a bus.

Americans believe that change is progress. Therefore, don't be surprised that there are fast changes in styles of dress and designs of cars.

However, some customs mentioned above may not be true in all parts of the USA. Customs in the USA are as different as the varied regions in this country. However, they are all different from my culture.

— Ha (Viet Nam)

EXERCISE (Cloze)

Fill in the blanks with *one* word that is correct.

Ha To has lived in (1) _____ only five months, but already (2) _____ has learned a lot about (3) _____ ways. She has learned that (4) _____ have to tell Americans how (5) _____ you are if you want (6) _____ get a job. She has (7) _____ that when friends eat together (8) _____ a restaurant, each one pays (9) _____ his own food. She has (10) _____ that often old people in (11) _____ don't want to live with (12) _____ children. She is not surprised (13) _____ see an American husband take (14) _____ of the baby and cook. (15) _____ is not surprised to see (16) _____ American wife drive a bus.

(17) _____ thinks that customs are different (18) _____ different parts of America. She (19) _____ all of the customs in (20) _____ are different from the customs (21) _____ her country.

Kimiko discovered that (22) _____ in San Francisco squeeze and (23) _____ to show "welcome." She was (24) _____ because she thought she knew (25) _____ little about American people. But (26) _____ had learned about American customs (27) _____ her sister-in-law, Sarah, who is (28) _____ Boston. Sarah never kisses to (29) _____ "welcome." Neither did Sarah's mother. (30) _____ in Boston are different from (31) _____ in San Francisco.

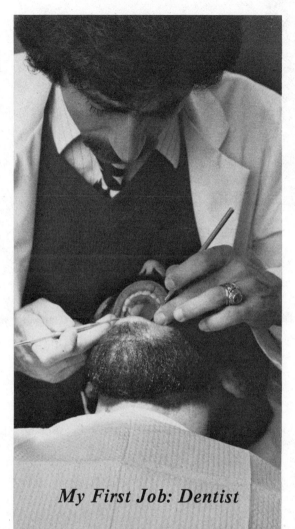

My First Job: Dentist

When I finished my university, I had to work two years for the Iranian Army as a dentist. So they gave me an office and I began to work. My first patient was a soldier. I wanted to pull out one of his teeth and I was afraid. I was afraid because when I worked in the university I had someone to help me. But now I was alone.

Finally, I got up my courage and pulled the tooth. It was a success! The tooth came out! From that day on things were easier for me in my first job.

— Ali (Iran)

My First Job: Teacher

My first job was the job of teacher. I taught some children six hours a day. I got paid $150 a month. I paid $30 a month for rent and $120 a month for food and clothes. But I couldn't live for $150 a month because everything was very expensive in my country. It is expensive all over the world now.

— Mohammed (Yemen)

My First Job: Seamstress

I'm 18 years old now. I have a job at a sewing factory. This is the first time I have worked.

I am working because now we have nothing. Also, my parents can't speak English so they can't get good jobs.

I don't like my job. My job is trimming clothes. I use a special machine. I work only part time, from 8 a.m. to noon, five days a week. I have been at this job since April.

After I finish my job, I come here and study. I'm looking for a new job which is better than the one I have now.

I decided I'll work just part time until my brothers come here. My first goal is to get a good job. These are my plans for the future.

— Rose (Greece)

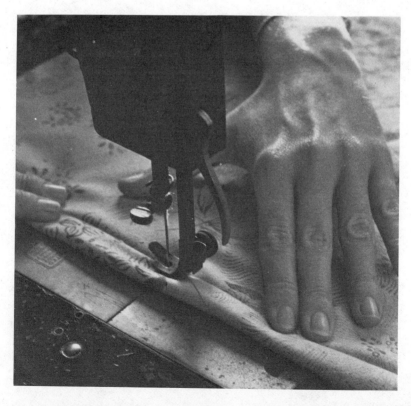

EXERCISE 1

Choose the correct answer: (a), (b), or (c).

1. In story 1, when Ali got his first job as a dentist, (a) he had already worked two years as a dentist for the Army, (b) he had never had a job as a dentist, (c) he had worked in his home town as a dentist.
2. Ali's first patient was (a) a small child, (b) an old woman, (c) a soldier.
3. Ali was afraid to pull the patient's tooth because (a) the patient was a friend of his, (b) Ali had too many people helping him, (c) Ali didn't have anyone to help him.
4. In story 2, Mohammed (a) could not live on $150 a month, (b) could live easily on $150 a month, (c) could live fairly well on $150 a month.
5. In story 2, Mohammed said that (a) things are not expensive in his country, (b) things are expensive all over the world, (c) things are more expensive in the U.S. than in Mohammed's country.

EXERCISE 2 (Writing)

Write two or three sentences about your first job. Say what you liked about it or what you didn't like. If you have never had a job, write about your father's, mother's, husband's or wife's job. Try to tell the interesting things about the job.

I Live in a House

I live in a house in the Avenues. I like to live in a private house because I am very comfortable.

The house is big and I can move with freedom. Then, if I am unhappy, sometimes I go out in my yard and I look at my flowers that I love very much. This makes me so happy.

If I live in an apartment, this doesn't happen. Then I have to be very careful of the people who live close to me. I won't know anybody well enough to make friends.

The doors in an apartment are close to each other. I should not make much noise because this might make somebody very nervous.

If one building has only two apartments, this is better than too many. Generally I don't like to live in an apartment. My life is more enjoyable when I live in a house.

— Hortensia (Guatemala)

EXERCISE 1

Choose one of these answers as correct (a), (b), or (c).

1. Hortensia lives in (a) a hotel, (b) a big house, (c) a big apartment.
2. She prefers (a) a large apartment but she can't find one, (b) to live in a house because she is more comfortable there, (c) to live in an apartment with her friends.
3. Hortensia thinks that apartments are (a) too noisy, (b) too expensive, (c) too unfriendly.
4. In her back yard, Hortensia has (a) flowers, (b) friends, (c) animals that she loves very much.
5. Apartment doors are often (a) right next to each other, (b) open and you can look in, (c) too far apart to make friends.

EXERCISE 2 (Writing)

Write two or three sentences about your house or apartment. Tell why you like it or why you don't like it. Do you prefer to live in an apartment or a house?

Escaping in a Small Boat

I was forced to leave my country in the winter of 1977. It was 10 o'clock at night when I began to get into the boat. The sky was dark and windy. I didn't know where I would go after my boat went into the open sea. Only the sky and sea were around me. The sea was dangerous because the waves were very high. I dared not look at them because I thought they could make my boat sink at any time.

Everybody on the boat was in a panic. Most of them were too afraid to do anything to save the boat from sinking. Just me and a few others were active. We silently bailed the water out of the boat so that the boat would not sink.

I felt very lonely and scared. I wished I could see something living or an island or a ship, but I couldn't see anything. I was very discouraged, and I don't know how to explain my feelings at that time.

But I never thought I would die, so after three days of tossing on the ocean, I got lucky. We saw a merchant ship of Norway. The sailors on the ship picked us up out of our boat and took us on board the ship. On the ship I lay down on the floor and said, "Thank God."

Now I could rest. There was no fear of sinking. No wars. No wind or shouting. I was in heaven.

— Diep (Viet Nam)

EXERCISE 1

Choose the correct answer: (a), (b), or (c).

1. Diep (a) had to leave his country, (b) wanted to leave his country, (c) wanted to come to the United States.
2. When Diep left his country (a) it was raining, (b) it was sunny, (c) it was windy.
3. On the boat, Diep was afraid (a) of sinking, (b) of not having enough to eat, (c) of the large fish in the ocean.
4. There was a lot of water in the bottom of Diep's boat so he and some other people (a) drank it because they were thirsty, (b) threw the water away from the boat, (c) put their feet in the water.
5. Diep kept looking for something while on the boat. He was looking for (a) an island, (b) a city, (c) a small town.
6. The writer of this story is (a) Cambodian, (b) Thai, (c) Vietnamese.
7. After three days on the boat, Diep and his friends saw (a) a ship, (b) an island, (c) a small boat tossing in the waves.
8. The ship (a) rescued the people on the boat, (b) sailed right by, (c) waved "hello" to the people on the boat.
9. When the ship picked up people from the boat, Diep (a) was scared, (b) was very thankful, (c) was very hungry and thirsty.
10. Diep felt that he could (a) take it easy on the ship, (b) work hard on the ship, (c) take a bath.

EXERCISE 2 (Writing)

Write about a time in your life when you were lonely and scared. What did you do?

24

Fog

Fog is like love;
It comes and goes
when you don't
expect it.
      — A student

The fog comes
on little cat feet.

It sits looking
over harbor and city
on silent haunches
and then moves on.
      — Sandburg

Fog

Fog is nice but not to me. It makes me sad when I see it. Then I think about all of my bad feelings. Some people are not near me, and I miss them when it is foggy.

I always think it comes because the sky wants to rain, and it feels just the same as me. We are both very unhappy. The fog is like a mirror. It shows my sadness to me.

— Mitra (Iran)

Fog

Fog is like smoke. It makes you sleepy. Sometimes it makes you daydream. I think of my home, my friends, and I miss my childhood. I see a white house in the forest. There is a hero riding on a white horse. Then the horse becomes faint.

Suddenly, there is the sun rising. Everything disappears. The time is up and I wake up.

— Sally (Hong Kong)

26

Fog

I had never seen fog before like the fog in San Francisco. But in my country we have a light fog on the surface of the Mekong River very early in the morning. And we have a fairy picture: Many small boats with lights float slowly on the river through the fog.

Some days, looking at the fog of San Francisco, I think I forget everything: The present and the past.

— Ngo (Viet Nam)

27

EXERCISE 1

Fill in the blanks with the correct form of the verb in parentheses. Use ONE word only.

Sally thinks that fog can (make) (1) _____ you sleepy. She (think) (2) _____ that sometimes it makes you daydream, too. When she thinks of home, she (miss) (3) _____ her childhood. She (see) (4) _____ a hero riding on a white horse in the forest. Then the sun (rise) (5) _____ and the picture of the hero and the forest (disappear) (6) _____ . Then it is time for her to (wake up) (7) _____ .

Mitra doesn't (like) (8) _____ fog. It can (make) (9) _____ her sad when she sees it. Then she (think) (10) _____ about her bad feelings. Does Mitra (feel) (11) _____ like crying when the sky looks like rain? Yes, she does. The fog will often (show) (12) _____ her her sadness.

Ngo (have) (13) _____ fog in his country on the Mekong River. It (come) (14) _____ very early in the morning. How do the boats (float) (15) _____ on the river, according to Ngo? Slowly. Some days in San Francisco, says Ngo, he can (forget) (16) _____ everything when he looks at the fog.

EXERCISE 2 (Writing)

Write a few sentences about some kind of weather in your country. For example, very hot or very cold weather, very rainy weather. What do you do in this kind of weather? Can you go out or do you have to stay at home?

WRESTLING

SWING

Kwong Bock Chol

HAN-BOTK

[1.]The festival's name is Kwong Bock Chol. [2.]We celebrate it at the foot of a mountain in every house of my country. [3.]We celebrate it on August 15. [4.]It is celebrated all day.

[5.]We don't have special costumes, but young and old women put on Korean clothes. [6.]The name of the Korean clothes is "Han-Botk."

[7.]There are two kinds of dances. [8.]One kind is danced by the young gentlemen and ladies. [9.]This is called a "folk dance." [10.]The other kind is danced by the old gentlemen and ladies. [11.]This is called the "village dance."

[12.]We don't build bonfires. [13.]We don't set off fireworks. [14.]We don't give presents to one another.

[15.]It is a time of fun and merry-making. [16.]The people, both young and old, men and women, join in celebrating the occasion.

[17.]I join in celebrating the occasion, too. [18.]I join in the dance, too.

[19.]People celebrate the festival because the nation of Korea was born on August 15. [20.]It isn't a religious feast.

— Sook (Korea)

EXERCISE 1

Make questions about the story above. (See example.)

Example: Make a question about the first sentence using the question word, "what."

What's the name of the festival?

1. Make a question about sentence 2 using the question word "where."
2. Make a question about sentence 2 using the question word "who."
3. Sentence 3 — when
4. Sentence 4 — when
5. Sentence 5 — what
6. Sentence 6 — what
7. Sentence 7 — how many
8. Sentence 16 — who
9. Sentence 19 — when
10. Sentence 19 — why

EXERCISE 2 (Writing)

Write a few sentences about a festival or a holiday in your country. For example, what is your favorite holiday and why? Or tell about one wonderful holiday when you were a child. What did you do that day?

MEMORIES

1.
The Best Smell

The best smell in the world for me is the smell of a special gum. It is made on a special date in a small town in Mexico. This town is the only town that makes it. There was a virgin who used to appear in the town. Her name was "Virgin de Talpa." The town is Talpa and the gum is called "chicle de Talpa" (Talpa gum). I would always like to have a piece of Talpa gum on my nose.

— Imelda (Mexico)

EXERCISE 2 (Talking and Writing)

First talk about different smells you like or dislike with one of your classmates. (Take 3 – 5 minutes to do this.) Then write a paragraph (three or four sentences) about the smell you remember most from your childhood.

2.
A Little Village in the Mountains

Many, many years ago I used to be a teacher. I taught for eight years. At the beginning, after passing a national test, they sent me to teach 30 children. It was in a very little village in the mountains in the north of Spain.

The area was extremely poor but beautiful. It was very green during the summer time and there was plenty of snow during the winter. The village was so little that it didn't have a doctor or a priest or even a mayor. There were only 30 families there and the only real authority was me.

At this time I was very young. I wanted to help people, especially children. I even thought I could change the world.

I spent one year there. I worked very, very much at school. It was a very hard year for me and I had a lot of experiences.

Sometimes I remember the things that happened to me that year, now so far away.

— Maria (Spain)

Roast Pig and Marinade
(A recipe)

Ingredients:
A 30 – 50 pound pig. This is enough for 60 to 80 people for a big party — usually a wedding.

Marinade:
    4 lbs. sugar
    1/2 gallon of soy sauce
    1 lb. of honey
    2 lbs. of soy bean
        preserves
    a little veisen powder
    1/4 lb. of garlic

(1)   Kill the pig. Take off the hair by boiling the pig in water. Then open the side of the breast and take out all of the insides. Clean and dry inside with a piece of cloth. Then hang the pig up to dry.

(2)   Peel the garlic and chop it in very small pieces. Then mix up all the marinade. Then put it into the chest of the pig.

(3)   Put the pig in a cool place for at least eight hours.

(4)   Then move the pig out and put it in a special stove at 500 degrees for about two hours.

(5)   Now eat the roast pig and marinade.

— Wong (Hong Kong)

34

EXERCISE 1

Use *how much* and *how many* in questions.

Example: How many people will a 30 – 50 pound pig serve?
It will serve from 60 to 80 people.

1. Ask how much sugar you need to make this roast pig.
2. Ask how many pounds of soy bean preserves you need.
3. Ask how much garlic you need.
4. Ask how long it takes to cool the pig.
5. Ask how much honey and soy sauce you need.

EXERCISE 2 (Writing)

Choose a recipe you like. Write how you make the recipe. If you cannot think of a recipe for food, then tell how to make a cup of tea or coffee. Explain how much dry tea or coffee, how much water, you need. And tell how long you wait before you drink the tea.

IF SPACEMEN CAME...

1.
If Spacemen Came...

If somebody came from another planet to my back yard, then I would do this. I would invite them to sit down, take it easy and rest for awhile.

I'd ask: "How was your trip?" "Where are you from?" I'd say: "Glad to meet you." "Please tell me if you'd like to see my country."

Then I'd ask: "Can I help you?" "Do you need transportation?" "Do you have some money?" "What are your favorite foods?" "Would you like something to drink?"

— Margaret (Poland)

2.
If a Spaceship Landed in My Back Yard...

If a spaceship from Mars landed in my back yard, I would make a special call to the police. And I would shout to my neighbor for help.

— Roberto (Mexico)

3.
If a Spaceshipman Came...

If a spaceshipman came to my house, I would open a bottle of Russian vodka. I would get drunk with the spaceshipman. Then I'd let him have a rest and the next day I would show him around my town.

— Vladimir (Russia)

4.
If a Spaceship Landed at My House...

If a spaceship landed near my house, I would run away from the spaceship. Then I would take my important papers and push them in a bag. Then I would call my daughter and husband from the house and run outside.

— Sonya (Russia)

EXERCISE 1 (Writing)

Write three or four sentences telling what you would do if a spaceship with space persons landed in your back yard.

EXERCISE 2

Make sentences with "if clauses."

Examples: (invite them to sit down) If spacemen landed in my back yard, I would invite them to sit down.

(take it easy) If spacemen landed in my back yard, I would tell them to take it easy for awhile.

(what about your trip?) If spacemen came to my house, I would ask about their trip.

1. (Where are you from?) If spacemen came to my back yard, I would _____ .
2. (Can I help you?) If spacemen came, I would _____ .
3. (Tell me about your country.) _____ .
4. (Do you need transportation?) _____ .
5. (What are your favorite foods?) _____ .
6. (Do you have some money?) _____ .
7. (Would you like something to drink?) _____ .
8. (I would call the police.) _____ .
9. (I would call my neighbor for help.) _____ .
10. (Would you like to see my town?) _____ .

FIRST IMPRESSIONS

Sweating in Court

Last month I got two $5 parking tickets on my car. It was not my fault. The meter was broken and I couldn't put any money in. Then about two weeks ago I got a letter. The letter told me that I had to go to court and pay the parking tickets. It was $10. I decided to tell the judge that it was not my fault.

I drove to the courthouse and it was very busy around the building. I couldn't find a place to park my car at 11:30 a.m. and the court was starting.

So I parked my car on the side of a small street that was not a very safe place to park. But I thought it would be O.K. for just a little time.

I was sweating when I arrived at the court. A little later the judge called my name. He said, "All right; you must pay the $10."

I explained to him that I should not pay because the meter was broken.

He said, "All right. You must pay."

I said I would pay. But I was unhappy. I thought the judge was not very kind.

Then I went back to my car. There was a new ticket on the window. Now I must pay $20 for the new ticket. And I still had to pay $10 for the first tickets.

— King (Hong Kong)

Wondering About American Men

In America, I find the customs between men and women very strange. For example, in Korea, my country, no men or women touch each other away from home. So I find the common sight in America of two people kissing or putting their arms around each other very hard to look at. Even holding hands in public is different from my way.

Also, in America, it is very difficult for me to know when people are telling the truth. I have seen a man come into a room and tell every woman he meets that she is beautiful. Surely not every woman is beautiful. So what does he mean? I think he means nothing if he says it to everyone.

Perhaps it is good to be open and to say at once what you think. Also, perhaps it is good to kiss someone in public if you truly love her. But I wonder in America if these are honest feelings. Sometimes kissing seems almost as casual as saying, "Hello." So I wonder how honest any American man can be.

— Kyong (Korea)

40

EXERCISE 1

Answer the questions in complete sentences.

1. When did King get his first ticket?
2. What was wrong with the parking meter?
3. Did King think it was his fault that he got the tickets?
4. When he went to the courthouse, where did he park his car?
5. Did he pay for the tickets in the courthouse?
6. What happened when he got back to his car?

EXERCISE 2 (Cloze)

Fill in the blanks with *one* word that is correct.

One time a student parked his car at (1) _____ parking meter. The meter didn't work. Later the (2) _____ found two parking tickets on his car. He went (3) _____ the courthouse to pay for them. He parked (4) _____ car on a small street. He went into the court. (5) _____ told the judge that the parking meter did (6) _____ work. The judge said that he must (7) _____ for the tickets anyway. The student went back (8) _____ his car and found a surprise. There (9) _____ another ticket on his car. This one was (10) _____ $20.

EXERCISE 3 (Talking)

In Korea men and women do not touch or kiss in public, so Kyong was surprised to see this in America.

1. How do you feel about kissing and touching in public?
2. Do friends — men and women — in your country often say "hello" or "goodbye" with a hug or a kiss or a handshake?
3. Do you feel uncomfortable when people get too close to you or touch you?

A Lovely Surprise

The first day I went shopping in America I had a lovely surprise. I went to the grocery store to buy my groceries for the next 10 days. I bought so many things that I couldn't carry them by myself.

I asked one of the workers if I could take the shopping cart out of the store to look for a taxi because my house is 15 blocks away from the store. The man told me that I could take the shopping cart to my house. I didn't understand him because my English was very bad, so I asked him again. He told me the same thing, "You can take the shopping cart to your home." Then I asked the manager. He said, "yes," too. I finally decided to take the cart home, because I couldn't find a taxi. I couldn't believe that they let people take shopping carts home. In my country it's impossible. The store would have called the police.

After pushing the shopping cart four blocks up Twin Peaks hill where I live, I stopped to rest. While resting, I saw a paper being carried by the wind. I caught it. It appeared to be a check. To my surprise it was a check — for $5,000! I thought it was a check that some business school used for teaching. But it looked good to me.

When I arrived home, I told my husband jokingly that I was rich. He asked me, "Where did you find the check?" I told him what had happened.

Later we went to the bank to find the owner of the check. Three days later I received a $10 reward with a beautiful letter telling me how honest I am.

The owner of the check was an old man who had moved from Arizona to San Francisco. While moving, he had lost the check. That check was his life's savings, so he was happy to get it back.

— Carmen (Mexico)

EXERCISE 4 (Writing)

Carmen was surprised that someone trusted her to take a shopping cart home. Do you think she felt good about being trusted? Have you ever been surprised when someone trusted you? How did it make you feel? Did you ever receive a reward for being honest? How did you feel about it? Write three or four sentences telling how you think being trusted or rewarded for honesty makes a person feel.

COMING TO AMERICA

Expectations

Before I came to the United States, I had so many beautiful hopes. I thought there were many good jobs. I thought that after a month's vacation I would get a job. I thought I could save a lot of money from my pay. First I would buy a new car made by General Motors. Then I would buy a house in the country. After a year, I would have my own business.

Then, every year, I would make enough money for a two months' vacation from my business. During that vacation I would go all around America.

I thought that there were many, many beautiful girls in the United States. It would be easy to find one, and I would marry her. That's what I thought.

Today is today. I have been here almost two years. But I am still a poor man. I still work for somebody. I am still not married and I drive a Ford car. Now I am feeling sad. But I still like the U.S.A.!

— Ho Kong (Hong Kong)

EXERCISE 1

Answer the following questions.

1. What did Ho think he would find in the United States?
2. Did Ho think he'd like to take a vacation after one month in the United States?
3. What did he decide he would do after he got a job?
4. Did he think he could some day afford a house outside of the city?
5. Would he travel around America?
6. What about finding a girl to marry? Did he think he would find one?
7. Is Ho married today?
8. Does he drive a General Motors car?
9. Does he work for himself?
10. What does he think about the U.S. today?

EXERCISE 2 (Writing)

Write a paragraph or two on what you thought you would find in America. What did you expect to do here? What do you expect to do in the future?

ANSWERS TO THE EXERCISES

Page

7 Ex. 1: 1. c; 2. a; 3. c; 4. a; 5. c; 6. a; 7. b; 8. a; 9. b; 10. c.

12 Ex. 1: 1. the; 2. —; 3. —; 4. The; 5. the; 6. The; 7. —; 8. the; 9. the; 10. The

16 Exercise (Cloze): 1. America; 2. she; 3. American; 4. you; 5. good; 6. to; 7. learned; 8. in; 9. for; 10. learned; 11. America; 12. their; 13. to; 14. care; 15. she; 16. an; 17. She; 18. in; 19. knows; 20. America; 21. in, 22. people; 23. kiss; 24. surprised; 25. a; 26. she; 27. from; 28. from; 29. show; 30. People; 31. people.

22 Ex. 1: 1. b; 2. c; 3. c; 4. a; 5. b.

24 Ex. 1: 1. b; 2. b; 3. c; 4. a; 5. a.

28 Ex. 1: 1. a; 2. c; 3. a; 4. b; 5. a; 6. c; 7. a; 8. a; 9. b; 10. a.

30 Ex. 1: 1. make; 2. thinks; 3. misses; 4. sees; 5. rises; 6. disappears; 7. wake up; 8. like; 9. make; 10. thinks; 11. feel; 12. show; 13. has; 14. comes; 15. float; 16. forget

41 Ex. 1: 1. a; 2. student; 3. to; 4. his; 5. and; 6. not; 7. pay; 8. to; 9. was; 10. for

NEWBURY HOUSE READERS

This series of books is for students of English. It is graded at six levels, from beginner to advanced. Structure and lexis are graded according to principles explained in the Newbury House Writers' Guide. The grading is flexible, so that the English is natural, though simple.

The lexical lists are a base. Extra words required by the context are used.

SUMMARY OF LEXICAL AND STRUCTURAL GRADING

Stage 1   **300 base words**
Present simple
Present continuous
Past simple (1)
Future, *going to*
Modals, *can* and *must* (1)
Imperatives
Questions (1, 2)
Indirect speech (1)
Determiners (1, 2)
And, but, or, because
Comparison and degree (1)
Elementary pronouns
    and possessives

Stage 2   **600 base words**
Future simple
Past simple (2)
Past continuous
Present perfect
Modals, *have to* (2)
Questions (3, 4)
Conditionals (1)
Indirect speech (statements) (2)
Determiners (3)
Relatives (1)
So (= therefore)
Comparison and degree (2, 3)

Stage 3   **1,000 base words**
Future continuous
Present perfect continuous
Past perfect
Modals, *may, ought/should* (3)
Passives (1)
Conditionals (2)
Reflexives (1)
Comparison and degree (4, 5)
Relative clauses (2, 3)
Indirect speech (questions, orders,
    requests) (3)
-ing words (1)

Stage 4   **1,500 words**
Past perfect continuous
Future perfect
Modals, *might, would rather/had better*
    (4)
Passives (2)
Conditionals (3, 4)
Determiners (4)
Comparison and degree (6)
Relative clauses (4, 5)
Indirect speech (*whether, unless*) (4)
-ing words (2, 3, 4)
Wish

Stage 5   **2,000 base words**
Future perfect continuous
Colored future
Conditionals (5)
-ing words (5, 6, 7)
Compounds with *-ever*
Relative clauses (6, 7)
Reflexives (2)
Such after negatives
Modals, *might/would have* (5)

Stage 6   **2,600 base words**
Modal verbs (6)
-ing words (8)
Impersonal forms
    (*it is said that.* . . . etc.)
Conditionals (6)
Relative clauses (8, 9)
Advanced connectors
    and conjunctions
Advanced noun clauses

Newbury House Readers provide a varied library for adult and high school students of English. They follow the principle that students learn most effectively when they enjoy learning. All the books, from mysteries to non-fiction, are entertaining and worth reading. Newbury House Readers are graded at six stages, from beginner to advanced. The vocabulary is based on a functional/notional syllabus, but also incorporates insights from frequency analysis. Grammatical structures are graded in an order that is consistent with major courses. Special provision is made for idioms, two-word verbs, affixes and words whose meanings can be deduced from known roots. All language, however simple, is natural. The grading is thus a flexible instrument which ensures both that the language is natural and that it is simple. All books contain comprehension questions and other language work to aid language mastery.

The *Newbury House Writers' Guide* explains the grading system in detail.

Other Newbury House Readers in this Series

Stage 1
THE LONG NIGHT, M. L. Allen
THE NIGHTMARE, Leslie Dunkling

Stage 2
GIFT OF THE MAGI and other American short stories, C. G. Draper
NEW YORK!, Warner Hutchinson
THE TIGER WITH THE BRIGHT BLUE EYES and other stories, Lewis Jones
DARKNESS BY THE RIVER and other stories, Lewis Jones

Stage 3
SOAP AND WATER, Linda Bosson
SUPERSTARS OF SPORTS, William Folprecht/Diane Lefer
BRIDGES TO FEAR, Mitsu Yamamoto
CALL OF THE WILD (Jack London), Mitsu Yamamoto
RED PENNY KING, M. L. Allen
PORTRAITS OF AMERICANS, Lewis Jones
MURDER IN THE LANGUAGE LAB, M. L. Allen

Stage 4
GREAT IDEAS!, Martha Ardiff/Eileen Seaward
THE DANGER LIGHT and other stories, Brian Harrison
THE OCEAN, Lewis Jones

Stage 6
LIFE, LIBERTY AND THE PURSUIT OF HAPPINESS,
   Mary Ann Kearny/James Baker